Teaching Kids to Care for God's Creation

REFLECTIONS, ACTIVITIES & PRAYERS
FOR CATECHISTS & FAMILIES

Mary Elizabeth Clark, SSJ

TWENTY-THIRD
PUBLICATIONS
twentythirdpublications.com

TWENTY-THIRD PUBLICATIONS
One Montauk Avenue, Suite 200
New London, CT 06320
(860) 437-3012 or (800) 321-0411
www.twentythirdpublications.com

Cover art: ©shutterstock.com/Eloku; ©shutterstock.com/cgterminal

ISBN: 978-1-62785-340-8
Library of Congress Control Number: 2017958806

Printed in the U.S.A.

 A division of Bayard, Inc.

CONTENTS

INTRODUCTION

Catholics have a spiritually significant reason to be deeply sensitive to how our common home of Earth is treated. It is a reflection of God. It is sacred. The elements we use in the sacraments are affected by how we treat Earth. Think about the water of baptism, the bread and wine of the Eucharist, oil for baptism, confirmation, anointing of the sick, and holy orders. We want all of these elements to be unsullied by pollution. How about the legacy we are passing on to our children and grandchildren? Will they be able to say of us that we did everything we could to change our ways so that our Earth could be healthy for them?

In this set of thirty sessions, we explore Pope Francis' encyclical *Laudato Si', On Care for Our Common Home* (LS). We are encouraged to pray with, think about, and act on ways to deepen our care for Earth.

Our home is no longer a safe place for life to thrive. God, through Pope Francis, is calling on us to do something about this situation before it is too late.

As you prepare your classes, I hope you will find the suggestions in this book useful. You might take a two-minute time slot at the beginning of class to give what could be considered a "spotlight" on caring for God's creation. You may choose to use the prayer as a closing prayer for the class. Additional ideas for children to share with their families are included with each lesson.

one

On care for our common home

"Praise be to you, my Lord, through our Sister, Mother Earth, who sustains and governs us." **LS, 1**

REFLECTION FOR CATECHISTS

Pope Francis says, "I believe that Saint Francis is the example par excellence of care for the vulnerable and of an integral ecology lived out joyfully and authentically" (LS, 10). St. Francis felt the oneness of all beings. Today, scientific advances help us to see that we are all part of one universe, and we are made of the same elements as the stars. We need to meditate on this reality and take it into our hearts. Our God is truly a God beyond all that is. Take time to be silent so as to listen to God speaking in your heart.

Pope Francis compares our love for our common home to the love between humans who fall in love with each other and want to do all they can to please and care for each other. St. Francis saw every creature as a brother or sister united to him by bonds of affection. That is why he felt called to care for all that exists. How can I begin to "fall in love" with our common home?

SUGGESTIONS FOR FAITH FORMATION

- Pope Francis chose his name to honor St. Francis of Assisi. St. Francis loved all creatures and especially people who were poor. Tell the story of St. Francis of Assisi and ask the children to make a drawing of their favorite part of the story.

- Have children name their favorite pet. Have the children take a photo of their pet and post the photos on the bulletin board.

- Show a picture of nature. Ask the children to tell you what they see. Ask them three times to look again to see if they see something new in the picture.

SUGGESTIONS FOR FAMILIES

- As a family, go on a nature walk. Talk together about how you each see God reflected in nature.

- What creatures in nature are your favorite? Have a family discussion about this.

- Plan an outing to a place where you can enjoy the gifts of God's creation. Take turns sharing what you enjoyed most about being outdoors.

- Find a place in your living room where you can set up a small "altar" of special things that can remind you of caring for our common home. Add special symbols and photos or pictures that help to keep your gaze on the beauty and wonder of creation.

PRAYER

Loving God, we thank you and praise you for the beauty in all of creation but most of all for _____ (each person says a favorite part of nature). Thank you for the beauty of our common home. Amen.

two

What is our common home?

If you don't know where you are, you don't know who you are.

RALPH ELLISON

Father Thomas Berry, a Passionist priest who died in 2009 at the age of 94, gave us a new understanding of the relationship between Earth and all living things. He taught that Earth is a living organism and thus filled with life. All other beings need to be in good relationship with Mother Earth in order to live in a healthy way. We may have lost our sense of place and thus no longer have a reverence for Earth. We are called by Pope Francis to find our way back home.

Think about the place where you live. What do you like most about it? Name some of the natural features of your yard or the land on which your home is located. How do you protect the natural surroundings of your home from damage or destruction?

- Explain to the children that the title of Pope Francis' encyclical on the environment is **Laudato Si' (On Care for Our Common Home)**. Invite the children to draw a picture of the earth "home" where they live. Encourage them to include the land formation, such as mountains, hills, valleys, rivers, lakes, and so forth. If possible, display the pictures in the parish under the banner "Our Common Home."

- Is there a history to the place you call "home"? Engage older children in researching the history of your geographical place. What happened many years ago in this place? Were there any indigenous people before others settled? Who were they? What are some practices of these native or indigenous peoples? Are there any streets or other places named for the First Peoples of this place?

- Explain that all forms of life are meant to have "homes." Use these questions to engage children in a discussion about homes for humans: *Do all humans have homes? What can you do for those who are too poor to have a home in your city, town, or village?* If possible, make arrangements for a visit to a local soup kitchen or food pantry.

- God has given us all a home on Earth. God wants all creatures to have a home. What can your family do to share this gift of God with other species of life? For instance, when you see insects or other small creatures, you can make sure they have a chance to live safely in their habitat.

- Work together as a family to create a terrarium for a small part of life to grow indoors. Find an empty jar. Layer small stones, charcoal, and soil at the bottom. Plant tiny rooted plants in it and add a few drops of water. Put a lid on it. You do not have to water it again. The microscopic organisms in the soil breathe out carbon dioxide and the plants produce oxygen for the full cycle of life to continue.

PRAYER

Loving Creator God, we praise and thank you for the beauty of our Earth, our one true home. We ask you to forgive us for how we have been thoughtless in caring for her. Amen.

three

What is happening to our home now?

The deterioration of the environment and of society affects the most vulnerable people on the planet. **LS, 48**

REFLECTION FOR CATECHISTS

Due to the rapid changes we humans have made to Earth, we have lost touch with nature. We may even lose touch with God, the Creator, who gave life to all things. This in turn causes great amounts of disconnection among humans and between humans and the environment. We can correct this by increasing our awareness. Awareness means taking a long, slow look at what happens around us.

One example of increasing awareness has to do with fresh drinking water. "Fresh drinking water," Pope Francis says, "is an issue of primary importance, since it is indispensable for human life and for supporting terrestrial and aquatic ecosystems. Sources of fresh water are necessary for health care, agriculture, and industry. Water supplies used to be relatively constant, but now in many places demand exceeds the sustainable supply, with dramatic consequences in the short and long term" (LS, 28).

- Life today is hectic and fast paced. We need to stop and listen to nature to learn how we ought to live. Listening is one way we will hear God's will for us. Perhaps we are missing the words of God because we are moving too fast. Give the students time at the beginning of class to breathe deeply. Invite them before class to count their breath in and out twelve times just to slow down and become more aware of their surroundings.

- Ask the children to describe the ways we use water. Emphasize how important it is for people to have access to fresh drinking water. Brainstorm ways to conserve water by doing things like shutting off the tap while brushing teeth.

- In order to be more aware of how we use water in our daily lives, we need to slow down and think about it. How aware are you of the amount of fresh water you use in a day?

- Explain how Pope Francis wrote about the importance of fresh water for all people in the world. Show what this means with the following demonstration about how little fresh water there is for all living things.

  Materials
  2 liter bottle = all water on Earth
  50 ml = fresh water on Earth
  Of this amount 35 ml trapped in glaciers

  Less than 1% of Earth's total water supply left for needs for agriculture, drinking, and washing as well as for lakes, rivers, and fresh water ecosystems.

SUGGESTIONS FOR FAMILIES

- In our home, there are many ways we can conserve water. For example, we can save the water that is used to rinse off dishes before putting them in the dishwasher by putting a dishpan in the sink and rinsing the dirty dishes in the pan first instead of running the water to rinse them.

- We can save water that has been used in the shower by placing a bucket in the shower to catch some of the running water. This can be used to water the flower garden. Be sure to use only biodegradable detergents and soap because this water goes into the ground water beneath the surface.

- Since you want to save as much water as possible, use only biodegradable soaps and detergents in the home. Biodegradable liquids can be absorbed in the ground water without causing harm to living things.

- Save rainwater by using a rain barrel outdoors. This water can be used to wash the car or to water the grass.

PRAYER

Loving Creator God, we praise and thank you for the beauty of our Earth, our one true home. We thank you for the precious gift of fresh water. Help us to be more aware of how we use water. Amen.

four

What can I do about pollution?

The Earth, our home, is beginning to look more and more like an immense pile of filth. **LS, 21**

Pope Francis reminds us that God has given us a beautiful home for all. There are many ways we are making our atmosphere unhealthy. The number of cases of asthma in children is increasing due to how careless we are in polluting the air. The atmosphere is a treasured gift that we all need to live. Planting trees helps to keep the air fresh because trees provide oxygen for the air. We can avoid burning fuels that create carbon dioxide, such as oil, coal, and gas, and instead use solar, wind, and geothermal forms of energy production. Take time to consider where the energy to fuel your home and provide electricity comes from and to make an effort to contribute to a cleaner planet. You might inquire from your energy company the sources of their energy. In some cases, you can make an additional contribution to them so that they will purchase the energy from solar or wind sources rather than from fossil fuels alone.

- Explain how pollution causes many unhealthy conditions for humans and other forms of life. Trees and plants die prematurely; cats and dogs suffer allergies. We can help to reduce pollution by using natural products for cleaning and personal care. Share the following ideas with the children and invite them to consider how they can contribute to a pollution-free world by bringing an idea home to implement with their families. Older children might research other ways to reduce pollution through individual and family efforts.

  » By using cloth napkins instead of paper napkins, we reduce the burning of trash that adds pollution to the air.

  » By reusing mugs and plates, we can reduce the amount of paper cups and plates used and thrown away.

  » Keeping as much as we can out of the landfill helps to reduce the amount of trash that ends up in incinerators. Incinerators burn fossil fuels that cause more pollution.

- Invite the children to make posters encouraging the three Rs of the environment: reduce, reuse, and recycle. Perhaps they can suggest three additional ones, i.e., re-imagine, replant, regenerate, renew, etc. Ask about posting the signs somewhere in the parish or school.

- Consider ways to change from toxic chemicals used for cleaning in your home to non-toxic materials. Vinegar, baking soda, and salt can be used for household cleaning purposes. Use the internet to find recipes for more healthy kinds of cleaning products and rid your house of toxic chemicals. For example, suggest that the students make a bottle of a natural cleaning product and bring it in to demonstrate how it works.

- Mix essential oils of lavender, peppermint, or lemon to a small amount of coconut oil for skin moisturizer.

- Consider alternative means of transportation, such as biking to work or riding public transportation. Combine shopping trips and other errands so as to use less gas.

- Set up a family contest to see who can use the least amount of fossil fuels in a week. Give a gift card as a prize.

PRAYER

Loving God, we thank you for the beauty of our Earth. Thank you for the blessings of fresh air and water. Amen.

five

Who lives in our common home?

*Every creature is thus the object of the Father's tenderness,
who gives it its place in the world.* **LS, 77**

REFLECTION FOR CATECHISTS

When we think about caring for others, those "others" must include
other species too. As humans, we must think about the consequences
our actions have beyond ourselves. Jesus did not consider his role as
Son of God something to be grasped only for himself but gave himself
as a human being so that we humans would know that God understands
us and loves us. We too must give of ourselves so that all other creatures
will also have life. How might we be considerate of the life forms other
than human that we may be affecting by our actions? Becoming more
conscious or aware will help us to notice the consequences of our actions
on those around us, both human and other species.

SUGGESTIONS FOR FAITH FORMATION

- As students enter your classroom, have music from different
  cultures playing. Ask the students to name the countries from
  which the music comes.

- What different cultures live in the neighborhood in which your parish or school is located? Engage students in identifying the places from which these cultures came.

- Prepare a snack using different cultural foods. Use colors of the flag for the country from which the food comes.

- Language is an expression of speech for communication among humans. Ask: *Do you know about the means of communication among other species? What means of expression do whales have? birds? reptiles? insects? dogs? cats?*

- Plan for a day to celebrate different cultures. Ask volunteers to bring a special dessert from their culture to share at the conclusion of class.

SUGGESTIONS FOR FAMILIES

- Pope Francis encourages us to remember to pray before and after meals as a way to care for creation. Use this time to highlight the gifts of each person in the family.

- When you join each other for a meal, be aware of how you are communicating with each other. Make meals a sacred time for the family to show love and support for one another while appreciating the food that nourishes your bodies.

- Mealtime can be an opportunity to practice manners. Being polite to one another shows how much we respect each other and do not want to offend each other. It takes a little more time to be polite but that time is well spent when we are showing love.

PRAYER

Loving Creator God, help us to become more aware of life in all of its forms. Show us how to be gentle to, and thoughtful of, each other in love. Amen.

Six

How do we live in our common home?

In some places, rural and urban alike,
the privatization of certain spaces has restricted people's access
to places of particular beauty. LS, 45

REFLECTION FOR CATECHISTS

God is present in every moment. If we just rush through our day, we may miss what God is trying to say to us. Contemplation has been defined as taking a "long loving look at reality." In *Laudato Si'*, Pope Francis says, "This contemplation of creation allows us to discover in each thing a teaching which God wishes to hand on to us, since 'for the believer, to contemplate creation is to hear a message, to listen to a paradoxical and silent voice'" (85).

Look closely at a rose and its features. What do you notice? Do this with three of your favorite flowers.

SUGGESTIONS FOR FAITH FORMATION

- Take time at the beginning of class to practice some form of quiet and reflective prayer.

- Here is a simple way to guide children in a quieting prayer:

  Close your eyes. Imagine you are sitting in a beautiful place near a lake or ocean. Coming close to you is Jesus. Jesus wants to be with you right where you are now. How does this feel? Invite Jesus to listen to what you want to say to him now. Speak to him about how you are feeling. If you have concerns on your mind, tell him about them. Let Jesus speak to you in response. Just be. At the end of your time, thank Jesus for being with you. Praise Jesus for always being there for you.

- Remind the children about how nature reflects God. The beauty of nature shows us a little bit about the beauty of God. Invite the children to reflect upon God's beauty. Ask them to share where they see the beauty of God in creation.

- St. Francis of Assisi noticed this beauty and praised God in song. Invite the children to create their own songs of praise to God for the beauty they see.

SUGGESTIONS FOR FAMILIES

- Take a family poll about some of your favorite places to view the beauty of nature. Plan a schedule of outings to each one.

- Create a place of beauty in your home to serve as a focus for family or individual prayer. This might be a garden shrine or a prayer table, using flowers, plants, rocks, and other signs of natural beauty.

PRAYER

Holy Family of Jesus, Mary, and Joseph, we ask you to help us as a family to understand each other better. Give us the graces we need to listen to each other with understanding, even when it is difficult. Amen.

Seven

What can I do about how I live in our common home?

Real relationships with others, with all the challenges they entail, now tend to be replaced by a type of contrived emotion which has more to do with devices and displays than with other people and with nature.

LS, 47

REFLECTION FOR CATECHISTS

How available is nature to you and your students? How can you create a way for them to experience nature in your area?

When we think about how we live in our common home, the works of mercy offer concrete guidelines. We can make a connection with care for creation and mercy. According to the *Oxford American Dictionary*, "mercy" is "refraining from inflicting punishment or pain on one within one's power." When we treat our Earth with compassion, we are merciful to her.

SUGGESTIONS FOR FAITH FORMATION

- Talk to the children about the meaning of mercy, and connect it with being merciful to Earth, our common home. Brainstorm ideas for showing environmental mercy through showing care for the Earth and its resources. Create a list to post in the classroom or another place in the parish.

- By becoming aware of those who lack the resources to live a healthy life, we learn that many people, both near and far, are in need of our merciful assistance. With the help of parents and parish staff, start a class collection of food or other goods for those in need. Help the children think about how they can be merciful in their thoughts and speech. Suggest that when they have a negative thought about a classmate, they can try to turn it into a kind thought about them.

SUGGESTIONS FOR FAMILIES

- In our Catholic tradition, there are many titles for Mary, the Mother of God. Look up the title "Our Lady of Mercy." What does it mean? Talk together about ways you can follow Mary's example and show mercy to one another.

- The Sisters of Mercy are a religious congregation of women in the Catholic Church. What can you find out about how they care for people who are materially poor?

PRAYER

Merciful God, we thank you for all the ways we see people showing mercy to each other. We thank you for the example of Jesus and his merciful way. Give us grace to increase our ways of showing mercy to all living beings. Amen.

eight

What does Jesus in the gospels show us about our common home?

In the Christian understanding of the world, the destiny of all creation is bound up with the mystery of Christ, present from the beginning. **LS, 99**

REFLECTION FOR CATECHISTS

Jesus calls us to love all of creation. He includes all creatures. Jesus lives in a loving manner with all of creation. When he met a person born blind, he wanted him to see. He healed him. We may not have the power to heal in a physical way, but we can be a healing presence in many ways. Reflect on one of your favorite biblical passages that shows how Jesus is a model for us of merciful healing. Read a biblical story from the gospels that illustrates how Jesus shows us how to treat others with mercy. For example, in the parable of the rich fool, Jesus shows the importance of sharing the goods of the earth (Luke 12:13–21).

SUGGESTIONS FOR FAITH FORMATION

- Explain to the children that Jesus calls us to greater trust in his heavenly Father, who will care for us. Ask: *What are some ways you can trust more deeply in God's care for you?*

- Invite the children to find an example of how Jesus used elements of nature in his teachings. Suggest that the children create a photo collage illustrating a parable or story from Scripture, for example, involving seeds or grains of wheat.

- The story of the multiplication of the loaves and fishes shows how Jesus took everyday food to teach about how we ought to share. Ask the students how we might share what we have with those who have less. Make a suggestion that the class bring a treat to share next week. See what happens if, by chance, someone forgets to bring the treat.

SUGGESTIONS FOR FAMILIES

- Join with other families to make meals to deliver to those who are homeless or homebound in your parish or neighborhood.

- As a family, decide to have "zero waste" celebrations by using only cloth napkins and reusable dishes. Eliminate the use of paper products, if possible. By collecting all the leftovers, Jesus gave us an example of using what we have and not wasting anything.

- Weigh your family's trash and decide how you as a family will reduce the amount of trash you create. Children can make this a contest by weighing the family trash for a week and seeing how much less they have created the following week.

PRAYER

Loving God, we thank you for sending us your Son Jesus, who became one of us in our common home here on Earth. We ask you to help us to become more like him in kindness and generosity. Amen.

nine

What can I do to be more like Jesus in how I live in our common home?

The Lord was able to invite others to be attentive to the beauty that there is in the world because he himself was in constant touch with nature, lending it an attention full of fondness and wonder. **LS, 97**

REFLECTION FOR CATECHISTS

Pope Francis reminds us that "Jesus lived in full harmony with creation, and others were amazed: 'What sort of man is this, that even the winds and the sea obey him?' (Mt 8:27)" (LS, 98). As you pay more attention to nature, you will learn lessons that will help you become more in harmony with all of creation. Think about how the trees sway with the wind. How does this idea help you to be more flexible? Think about how the squirrel goes about the business of preparing for winter. How does this behavior of the squirrel help you to plan ahead?

SUGGESTIONS FOR FAITH FORMATION

- Explain to the students how humans have removed themselves from nature over time and how the effects of that removal are harming our way of being in harmony with each other and with nature. Give some examples, such as the constant use of cell phones and technology. Although there are good uses of technology, it can get in the way of our being in tune with nature. Talk about what it would be like to go without using a cell phone for a day. What would make it hard?

- Make two lists, one list for the good uses of technology and the other for how technology can harm our relationships. Lead a discussion with the students about the lists.

- Go outside and find something in nature (i.e., a blade of grass, a leaf, a flower petal, etc.). Ask the students to draw as much as they can see in that piece of nature. Explain that we often miss how intricate the beauty of nature is because we rush past it.

SUGGESTIONS FOR FAMILIES

- Create times for your family to spend outdoors.

- Visit the local zoo as a family. What are some ways the zoo is caring for the animals?

- Visit a local nature center. Learn the names of the trees that are native to your area. See if you can identify these trees on a nature walk in your neighborhood.

- Plant a tree as a family and dedicate it to one of your family members who has died.

PRAYER

Jesus, loving Savior, you lived in harmony with nature and can teach us to do the same. Please give us your patience, serenity, and grace. Amen.

ten

What does my faith teach me about how to live in our common home?

Our very contact with nature has a deep restorative power;
contemplation of its magnificence imparts peace and serenity.
SAINT JOHN PAUL II, MESSAGE FOR WORLD DAY OF PEACE, 1990

REFLECTION FOR CATECHISTS

St. John Paul II helps us to realize the beauty in nature and its healing power. He says the more time we spend in nature the better we will be. Today, we sometimes lose time outdoors due to the increased time we may spend at the computer or within the confines of our workplace or home. Pope Francis and St. John Paul II have both encouraged us to appreciate the effect nature can have on us physically and mentally.

What can you do each day to spend some time outdoors? Perhaps you can park the car a distance from your destination just to get a little more time walking out of doors. Take a short walk around the block during your lunchtime. Be more conscious of the beauty out the window of your car, bus, train, and home. Deepen your attention to what little signs of nature appear in your environment. Use a calendar to check off how much time you spend outdoors each day.

SUGGESTIONS FOR FAITH FORMATION

- Open your lesson with a moment outdoors, if possible. Open the windows and let the fresh air flow through the room. Breathe deeply. Gaze at a single flower or a tree nearby. Ask God to open your eyes to the beauty of the tiniest insect or a blade of grass.

- Appreciating the smallest aspects of nature helps us to appreciate the smallest ways that God can speak to us. Remind the children that God is present in every bit of nature and in every bit of their bodies, minds, and spirits. God is present in every part of our day. We can know that presence just by being aware.

- Contemplation has a deep history in the church, both western and eastern traditions. Some holy persons known for teaching how to contemplate are Benedict, Scholastica, Francis of Assisi, Clare of Assisi, Teresa of Ávila, Thérèse of the Child Jesus, Gregory the Great, and Julian of Norwich. Ask each member of the class to research one of these persons. Tell them to be prepared to share what they found to be most interesting.

SUGGESTIONS FOR FAMILIES

- Set up a home prayer corner with an altar of sacred images that help the family to focus on prayer. This could include a crucifix, a statue of the Blessed Mother, pictures of ancestors who have gone before us to heaven, a rosary for each family member, and a candle. (Safety precaution: use a candle that runs on batteries.)

- Set up a music player for soft, meditative music that you can play before you begin your family prayer time. Sit together for a moment of silent prayer.

- Practice ways to deepen your awareness of God's beauty in creation. Have photos of nature from places you have visited.

- Sing a hymn that praises the beauty of creation. For example, use "All Creatures of Our God and King" by St. Francis of Assisi, or another song found in your church hymnal.

- Plant a flowering bush in memory of a relative who has died. Plant it on their birthday.

PRAYER

Loving God, Three-in-One, we adore you and we praise you as we join in prayer for all of creation. Give us the courage to do what we know can be inconvenient but necessary to care more deeply for your creation. Amen.

eleven

What does science teach about our common home?

Science and religion, with their distinctive approaches to understanding reality, can enter into an intense dialogue fruitful to both. **LS, 62**

Pope Francis reminds us that there are many facets to the ecological crisis and its multiple causes. He says we will not find solutions in only one facet. We can look to science to teach us much about the causes of the damage done to our atmosphere, waters, and land. We respect the time and talent that have gone into the study of these causes.

There are Catholic scientists who have studied the origins of the universe. They tell us it goes back fifteen billion years. They say the same elements found in the stars and at the beginning of the universe are also found in us. We are all one in our basic elements. What a wonderful thought! Jesus' desire that we may all be one is a reality in this scientific fact. Praise be the Creator who made us all one. How does this make you feel? Do you wonder at the mystery of God? Does this help you to understand how awesome God is? Let this awesomeness move through you so that you can communicate it to the children. Enthusiasm, which means "filled with God," is a sign that we are in awe of God. Show the children how filled with God you are by your enthusiasm about God's creation.

SUGGESTIONS FOR FAITH FORMATION

- Before Pope Francis became a priest, he had studied chemistry. So he had a knowledge of science and respected it. He mentions how "exposure to atmospheric pollutants produces a broad spectrum of health hazards, especially for those who are poor." He has compassion for those who are materially poor and unable to escape from hazardous pollution. How do we show our compassion for those who are getting asthma in our own country due to poor air quality?

- Tell the children how Pope Francis studied chemistry. Emphasize his understanding of and respect for science and what it teaches us about our Earth and the universe. Engage older children in a discussion of the different kinds of science that teach us about the Earth. Make a chart listing these (biology, zoology, climatology, and so forth).

- Compile a list of questions the students would like to know about Earth and the ways we can care for the environment. Divide the class into small groups, and assign each group a question to research together. If desired, compile the results on posters and place in the parish along with a prayer of thanksgiving for the gift of God's creation.

- Science in all of its various dimensions is quite complex. We applaud the research by scholars over many years that have given us the antibiotics and vaccines to eliminate some diseases that were often fatal in the past. Find the names of scientists who have made a discovery to help cure a disease. For example: Albert Schatz found the antibiotic that could cure tuberculosis. Although we may not be able to cause a miraculous change as Jesus did, we can contribute to healing in our own region.

SUGGESTIONS FOR FAMILIES

- Ask your children what they are learning in science class. How does their faith connect with what they are learning? Are there questions concerning issues of faith that you can discuss as a family?

- Show respect and reverence for the science of space and the origins of the universe. We believe that God is Creator of all that is. Science can help us to appreciate God even more, because we cannot understand a mystery like the creation of the universe. So, no matter how the universe came to be, we believe it is God who made it possible. When scientific discoveries help us to better understand how God's creation came into being, that is good. Engage in a discussion about the ways science has contributed to the safety and well-being of your family.

PRAYER

Loving God, Creator of all that is, be with us as we explore your magnificent creation. We beg you to help us when we fail and to give us the courage to live together in peace and harmony. Amen.

twelve

What do I know about the mystery of the universe and our common home?

In the Judaeo-Christian tradition, the word "creation" has a broader meaning than "nature," for it has to do with God's loving plan in which every creature has its own value and significance. **LS, 76**

Astronomers have uncovered enormous amounts of information about the evolution of our universe. We in the twenty-first century are the beneficiaries of this wonderful research and discovery. As people of faith, we can deepen our understanding of God, the Creator of such awesome wonders. The history of the universe can now be traced back more than fifteen billion years. We have the scientific evidence for understanding more about what the stars are made of and how we humans are made of the same elements. So, in fact, we are all one! This also calls us to be more responsible for what we know. We are called to love all of creation.

- Talk to the children about how the Earth is home to millions of other species of life. We believe that Jesus Christ, the Son of God, was born to be like us in all things but sin. In doing so, Jesus gave us the best example of how we need to live gently, simply, and lovingly with all life-forms, especially the human. Invite the children to discuss in small groups or write about ways we can follow Jesus by living simply and lovingly with others.

- Ask the students to give an example of what it means to live in the "spirit of the law" and not only the "letter of the law." Describe the following scenario and invite their responses: *You are walking home from the store and you see an older person struggling with a package of groceries. You know you are already late for supper. What do you decide to do?*

- Talk about the church's teaching on the dignity and worth of every person. Explain how some people mock those who have difficulty speaking a second language. This is unloving and hurtful. Emphasize the decisions we can make to understand those who are trying to speak a language that is not their own, especially when it may sound unusual.

- Brainstorm the challenges that people with physical or mental disabilities face. Discuss ways to treat all people with compassion and kindness.

SUGGESTIONS FOR FAMILIES

- Find photos of the universe to put on your family prayer table.

- Now we know we are made of "stardust." Use a small container of sparkles to represent stardust as a symbol of our unity with all of creation. Put a pinch of the sparkles into each person's hand. Go outdoors to sing a hymn of praise and sprinkle them into the air.

- Before and after meals, pray in thanksgiving for those who farmed the land, prepared the meal, and placed it on our table. Also, pray for those who do not have enough to eat this day. For example: "Loving God, we pray for all those who worked hard in the fields to make our food possible. We thank you for all that is before us and for those who helped prepare it. We are mindful of those who are not eating tonight and ask you to bless them. Amen."

PRAYER

Holy Spirit of the universe, we thank you for the awesome beauty of our Earth and of all that surrounds us in the universe. All are one! Help us to live in such a way that others see our belief in our unity. Amen.

thirteen

What can I learn from nature and our common home?

Soil, water, mountains: everything is,
as it were, a caress of God. **LS, 84**

REFLECTION FOR CATECHISTS

Nature teaches us so much! When we gaze with loving eyes, we see how gently trees sway in the wind, flowers bloom in the spring, and waves flow toward the beach. There are rhythms of gentleness that we can learn from the seasons and the tides. Pope Francis compares nature to a caress of God. What are some ways that you can appreciate this caress? Take time to reflect on your favorite parts of nature. What might you do to protect this caress of God through wise environmental practice?

SUGGESTIONS FOR FAITH FORMATION

* Share the quote by Pope Francis about soil, mountains, and sea being a "caress of God." Distribute paper and markers and invite your class to draw a landscape that shows the beauty of God's creation. Create a collage by hanging the pictures together.

- Make small bags for carrying a water bottle so it can be refilled, rather than using bottled water. Look up the reasons why using bottled water is not good for Earth.

- Ask volunteers to research the meaning of the word "biodegradable" and to share their findings with the rest of the class.

SUGGESTIONS FOR FAMILIES

- Find out how to measure your "carbon footprint" online. As a family, calculate your carbon footprint and decide what you can do to reduce the amount of carbon dioxide or methane that you are putting into the atmosphere.

- Explain how the production of red meat for consumption in our country causes damage to the Amazon rainforest. Think about why this is important to understand.

- Look up the causes of methane in the atmosphere. Discuss why eating less red meat reduces methane in the air. Begin a practice of meatless Mondays or meatless Fridays.

- Discuss ways to eliminate or reduce the use of paper as much as you can. For example, use cloth napkins and towels.

PRAYER

Holy Spirit of light and love, pour upon us your graces of courage and strength. Help us to wake up to how we are behaving so that all creatures sharing our common home may continue to live. Amen.

fourteen

What are some ways I can be more creative in living in harmony with all of creation?

Faced with the widespread destruction of the environment, people everywhere are coming to understand that we cannot continue to use the goods of the earth as we have in the past...a new ecological awareness is beginning to emerge...the ecological crisis is a moral issue.

SAINT JOHN PAUL II, MESSAGE FOR THE WORLD DAY OF PEACE, 1990

REFLECTION FOR CATECHISTS

Creativity reflects God's nature within each of us. Each of us, like pieces of a puzzle, can contribute to the beauty of the whole by sharing our different gifts. Each person is needed for the whole picture. Diversity is how God created nature and us. No reason to be competitive. We can cooperate to make everyone happy.

Let your imagination open itself to the many varied ideas possible. As a catechist, you model creativity. What is your particular gift of creativity? How can you show God you appreciate it?

- Demonstrate creativity with your students by giving each one an empty box (of varied sizes). Suggest that they decorate their boxes with magazine pictures of nature. Because each person has a different favorite thing in nature, the boxes will all be different. Invite them to take the boxes home to share with their families. They might use them to collect prayer intentions to pray before meals or bedtime.

- Have the students in groups of two imagine themselves as a species other than human in nature. Ask: *What about this species attracts you? What about this species makes you want to imitate it? Are you able to imagine how you would imitate this species in a good way? Are you able to formulate a prayer that reminds you of this species?*

- Compose a prayer of three or four lines beginning with "Loving God,...." For example: "Loving God, thank you for creating life in so many different ways. Help me to appreciate the many different ways you created humans, too. Amen."

- Go outside and look for trees to observe with your group. Invite your students to choose a tree to observe more closely. Ask: *What do you like about this tree? Does it have a particular shape of leaf? What about the bark?* Share with the group what each person likes. How are the aspects of the tree different?

- Think about the many gifts each of the members of your family offers. Imagine a way that you can affirm these gifts. For instance, invite each member of the family to write out one of their gifts and post it on a family bulletin board. This helps other members of the family to affirm the gifts of each other. For example, Susan has the gift of photography. She takes a photo of a favorite place for the birthday person. She has it framed or makes a frame for the photo as a gift.

- At a birthday celebration, share your individual family gifts as a way to express your love for each other. Perhaps you could hand-make the decorations. Make recycled cloth pennants instead of buying paper decorations. Offer to celebrate the birthday in a place where you can appreciate nature. Or, put on a simple family show for the birthday person.

PRAYER

Creator God, father and mother of us all, we praise and thank you for the variety we experience in nature. Give us the grace to accept your gifts within ourselves and to share what we have with each other. Amen.

fifteen

How can I practice being in harmony with all life?

*The universe as a whole, in all its manifold relationships,
shows forth the inexhaustible riches of God.* LS, 86

REFLECTION FOR CATECHISTS

Practicing peaceful interdependence with all of life draws us closer to
our Creator God and to one another—all humans as well as all other
species. A life of peace and nonviolence is rooted in the heart of love.
Within each of us is a mirror reflection of the God of love. Language is
one way we express love and nonviolence. We can transform our language and see how it helps to change our behavior.

As we know, language can shape our reality in ways we may be
unaware of. So, awareness of the meaning of our words can shift our
behavior and actions. For example, we can stop using a phrase like
"Shoot me" because of its violent meaning. We can use another expression like "I hope that never happens to me." Small changes like this can
make a big difference in our understanding of how we can transform
our world from one of violence to one of harmony.

- Teaching practices of peace rather than violence can be interactive with students. Place objects that could be perceived either as tools for peace or for violence on a table. Hold them up one at a time. For example, ask the students how a hammer is used for peace and how it can be used for violence. Other examples to use: scissors, a match, or water. Just as these things can be used for good or for evil, we too can act for good or for evil. We need the grace of God to help us to live in harmony and to act for good.

- Brainstorm words that convey courtesy and gratitude. For example, use the words "Please" and "Thank you" every time you want something and then get it.

- Ask the students to think of all the words they hear or use that have a violent meaning. Ask them to think of ways they can switch to another word. For example, when we want to express our anger, we can do so in a way that does not add more violence to the situation. By counting to ten we can help ourselves calm down before saying anything.

- Play soothing music to give an atmosphere of calm to the room. For example, use a relaxing piece of classical music. Invite the students to draw a calming picture as they listen. Use a chime or soft bell to return from discussion groups to quiet in the room.

SUGGESTIONS FOR FAMILIES

- Playing with toys can be a way to teach peaceful behavior to children. Show by example how working together makes for happiness and joy. For example, forming teams that play cooperative games rather than competitive games can illustrate this concept. Look up games of cooperation on the internet. Play one of these games at home.

- One way to practice cooperation is by cooking a meal or baking bread together. Assign each person a task and affirm the ways in which everyone works together. When enjoying the food, give thanks for the gift of harmony in your home.

- Reward your children for cooperation and harmony rather than competition. Show how "getting along" will increase positive energy in the world. Encourage fair and nonviolent behavior in sports or other competitive activities. Give an example of what it means to be a "good sport."

- As a group with other families in your neighborhood or parish, plan a cooperative effort of donating food to a local food pantry or soup kitchen.

PRAYER

Mary, our mother, we ask you to help us to learn how to live in harmony with each other and with all of the other species on our earth. We want to be more peaceful in our family. Help us to imitate you in providing a safe and peaceful home for all of God's creatures. Amen.

Sixteen

How do I get along with people who do not agree with me?

A sense of deep communion with the rest of nature cannot be real if our hearts lack tenderness, compassion, and concern for our fellow human beings. **LS, 91**

REFLECTION FOR CATECHISTS

Most times, we may get along with each other—at home, at school, and at play. But once in a while we might disagree with someone. It is important to learn how to work through our disagreements.

In order to get along with others, especially those who disagree with me, I need to step back and take a breath before speaking with them. I need to tell myself how God loves this person even though I may not understand them right now. In every person as well as in myself, there are good and not so good characteristics. Some personalities clash with others. Not all people find me easy, and I may not find all persons easy to accept. So, my first step toward peaceful conversation is to decide that I do not need to speak so much. I need to listen more frequently. This calms me down so my fear of the other is not so strong or unconscious. I am more aware of my need for breathing deliberately.

Step One: Count to ten.

Step Two: See the person as God sees them—with love.

Step Three: Invite the other person to a conversation. For example, say, "May we talk?"

SUGGESTIONS FOR FAITH FORMATION

- Emphasize the value of communicating peacefully and respectfully with others. Divide the class into small groups and invite each group to create a role-play in which people disagree. Encourage them to think of creative ways to communicate in a peaceful and respectful way. After the groups present their role-plays to the rest of the class, invite responses and further ideas for respectful communication.

- Brainstorm a class list of words and attitudes that promote peace and show respect for one another. Post the list by the prayer table or in another prominent place and add to it as the class further develops an awareness of respectful communication.

- Plan to have family gatherings/meetings once a week, perhaps on Sunday night, to check in with each other about how you are each doing. Agree to speak about your feelings with care and sensitivity in the family meeting. This will help to address anything that is disturbing the peace before it gets too big.

- Do not let negative feelings fester, or they will only get worse. Consider ways to increase the time you spend listening to one another. Eliminate distractions when working out a family disagreement so that you can pay close attention to what each person is saying and feeling.

- Share what is going on with you so your family members know about what you are doing. By sharing, you show you care about them.

PRAYER

Loving Parent God, father and mother, you are our hope in times of trouble. Come to our aid to help us to share with each other when we are feeling sad or alone. Show us how to be compassionate and merciful to each other when we disagree. Amen.

Seventeen

Steps to making a decision to keep the peace

Our freedom fades when it is handed over to the blind forces of the unconscious, of immediate needs, of self-interest, and of violence. **LS, 105**

We assume that all people want to live in peace. However, sometimes there are circumstances that cause a disruption in the peace. So we need to become aware of the consciousness of decision making. Before we keep making assumptions, thinking that peace will just happen, let's look at what we need to do to achieve peace.

Making a decision takes skill. There are several steps in the process of decision making.

> ***Step One:*** Brainstorm with anyone else who is interested in the outcome of the decision, especially those who will be directly affected by it.

> ***Step Two:*** Discuss the pros and cons of the choice you hope to make. This is the time for speaking up and giving the positive and negative possible outcomes.

Step Three: Decide who will make the final decision.

Step Four: Decide how the decision will be carried out and by whom.

Step Five: Make the decision and clearly announce it. All must accept the outcomes of the decision and support its accomplishment.

Once the decision has been made, all must abide by it according to the ground rules.

SUGGESTIONS FOR FAITH FORMATION

Peacemaking with each other helps with peacemaking with Mother Earth. Everything is interconnected; thus we need to be aware of how every action we as humans take has its effect on others. Technological advances have been valuable when they have been carefully studied and shown to cause no harm.

- Invite students to discuss the following questions: How do you see technology used respectfully? How is it used disrespectfully? Are there ways that you use technology to deepen your connections not only to humans but also to other species? For example, in science, how is technology being used to give better health to humans as well as to other species? Invite volunteers to research this question and return to class with some examples.

- Brainstorm a list of the ways your students might peacefully move through differences or disagreements. Invite students to reflect upon ways to "keep the peace" with Mother Earth. Ask them to write or draw their responses and then share them with one another.

SUGGESTIONS FOR FAMILIES

Home ground rules can help to set the boundaries at the beginning of the year.

- Create an artistic poster for the family to express your rules. Post it in a common place for all to see and to be reminded of the agreement you have made together for living in peace and harmony.

- Make a list of steps that your family agrees to use for peaceful problem solving.

- Reward each other with age-appropriate simple prizes when someone makes a change from negative to positive behavior. This can reinforce it.

- To show your love, offer to do chores that seem difficult for others in your family.

PRAYER

Loving God, we praise and thank you for all your gifts to us. Especially, we thank you for the love we feel as a family. Help us to forgive each other and to move past our hurts. Amen.

eighteen

How does technology help me to care for our common home?

Neglecting to monitor the harm done to nature and the environmental impact of our decisions is only the most striking sign of disregard for the message contained in the structures of nature itself. **LS,117**

REFLECTION FOR CATECHISTS

Our faith teaches us to care for God's creation. Today, with the abundance of technological advances, we can be overwhelmed by the speed with which we can do things. However, there is a danger to thinking "more is better" or "faster is better." The practice of meditation can slow us down so that we can better listen to what is going on inside of us. In prayer, we speak to God, and we listen to what God is saying to us as well. In order to hear what God is saying to us, we need quiet time to slow down and listen with our hearts.

Pope Francis knows the consequences of overdoing our use of technology; it can keep us so distracted from life around us that we fail to notice each other and nature. He calls us to become more consciously aware of how we use technology. We must not allow ourselves to be controlled by it; rather, we need to take control of it and use it for the good of others and nature.

SUGGESTIONS FOR FAITH FORMATION

Use the following exercise to open your class session:

- Take five minutes to stop and listen in silence at the beginning of the lesson.

- Invite the children to gaze at an image of God that helps them focus. Provide images that have traditionally been used to represent Jesus, such as the Good Shepherd, the Sacred Heart, Jesus and the children, etc.

- Use a gong or chime to draw the children out of the silence. End the time with a brief mantra such as "Jesus, you are so good to me" or "Jesus, you give me help."

SUGGESTIONS FOR FAMILIES

- Use the internet to find special prayers for the season, such as a guided meditation.

- Create a poem or prayer, and email it to a family member who lives alone or is ill.

- Create a booklet of prayers.

- Use a template from a collection on the computer that helps you to make a booklet of special quotes that remind you of the wonder of nature.

PRAYER

All Holy One, we ask you for wisdom to use the technology we have in ways that bring us closer to you. Give us the grace to only use technology for your honor and glory. Amen.

nineteen

What does food have to do with our common home?

The community of believers was of one heart and mind,
and no one claimed that any of his possessions was his own,
but they had everything in common. **ACTS 4:32**

REFLECTION FOR CATECHISTS

When we read Scripture, we learn how the first community of believers lived in imitation of Jesus and his teachings about love. Today, the Christian community includes many more people than in the earliest days of Christianity. We are challenged to find new ways to share our possessions with those in need. Food, a basic necessity for life, could be a theme for developing a series of lessons on how to live in community with more ethical principles.

Use the following questions to reflect more deeply on the food you consume:

- Where does our food come from?

- How much gas did it take to bring it to our table?

- Who are the people who picked the food? Grew it? Do they live in decent housing?

- What about people who live in other parts of the world? For example, how about people in Somalia?

- What am I doing to promote thoughtfulness about others who are hungry?

SUGGESTIONS FOR FAITH FORMATION

- Discuss the importance of locally grown produce in your area. Engage the help of parent volunteers to prepare a small meal of locally grown food. Begin and end the meal with prayers of thanksgiving for those who grow and bring to market the food we eat.

- Cultivate a small herb garden in the classroom. Engage the children in planting seeds and tending the plants as they grow.

- Learn about how Catholic Relief Services provides food for those who are hungry in other countries. Invite your parish to participate in the program called "Helping Hands."

- Catholic Relief Services has films for educational purposes. These films help to make concrete the reasons for almsgiving and fasting during Lent.

- Create a shrine to St. Francis of Assisi with a small garden around it. Grow vegetables or flowers to share with those who are homebound.

- The word "agape" refers to the early Christian meal the community used to celebrate the love of the group. It was not the same as the eucharistic meal; it was in addition to the eucharistic liturgy. Today, the agape meal can be a way to celebrate a small Christian group such as a class or a family. Because a meal is one of the best ways we have to come together as a family, we can celebrate an agape meal as a family during a religious season such as Advent, Christmas, Lent, or Easter. Suggest that for this agape meal you will use locally grown food to support local farmers and gardeners.

- Suggest that the family plant its own garden of vegetables (i.e., tomatoes, peppers, cucumbers, etc., for a salad). Choose plants that are indigenous to your area. Begin with a raised bed garden that is easy to control. In urban areas you can plant vegetables in large flower pots or containers. Growing our own vegetables helps us to appreciate real food and how much work goes into growing it.

PRAYER

Loving God of all the universe, we thank you for all the food you provide for our nourishment of body, mind, and spirit. Help us to use our body, mind, and spirit to glorify you in everything we say and do. Amen.

twenty

What kind of games can deepen our care for our common home?

Care for nature is part of a lifestyle which includes the capacity for living together and communion. **LS, 228**

REFLECTION FOR CATECHISTS

To create harmony and peace, we need more cooperation in communication. Games based on cooperation encourage harmony and peace. This strengthens the notion that care for creation can be fun.

SUGGESTIONS FOR FAITH FORMATION

- Assemble mobiles for the classroom. Small groups can work on a theme from Pope Francis' ***Laudato Si'***. Examples:

  1. We keep our Earth home clean.
  2. We save our fresh water.
  3. We protect trees and plant life.
  4. We care for creation so all people who come after us will also enjoy it.

- Use old magazines for pictures to illustrate the themes. Assemble the mobiles, using recycled straws and hangers with string to hang them from the ceiling.

- On the Feast of St. Francis of Assisi (October 4) invite everyone to sign the St. Francis Pledge. Go to *www.catholicclimatecovenant. org*. Form small groups to carry out the following tasks:

  1. find out what signing the pledge requires of you;
  2. make an appointment with the pastor or principal to seek permission to make the pledge;
  3. make copies of the pledge for each person. Once you have received permission, go to the website and sign in for your parish or school.

SUGGESTIONS FOR FAMILIES

- Have a family fun and games night. Have several board games available. Make it intergenerational.

- Create a prayer box for the family. Decorate it and make it special with attractive artwork. Put the special prayer intentions each member of the family carries in his or her heart in the prayer box. Be sure to add prayers for our Mother Earth. At prayers before meals, take out one prayer intention and pray for that intention together. Add slips of paper with prayer intentions on them anytime during the week.

PRAYER

Loving triune God, as a community yourself, you model what it means to be a loving presence in the world. Help us to learn how to live together in harmony and peace. Amen.

twenty-one

What would a new way of being look like for our common home?

The ecological crisis reveals the urgent moral need
for a new solidarity, especially in relations between the developing
nations and those that are highly industrialized.

SAINT JOHN PAUL II, WORLD DAY OF PEACE MESSAGE, 1990

REFLECTION FOR CATECHISTS

Because we live in a fast-paced society, we need to relearn "how to just be." A "way of being," unlike a "way of doing," calls for us to quiet ourselves to such a degree that no amount of thinking, acting, or doing exists in our behavior. Rather, we simply are! How does that feel? That is how God accepts and loves us. We need to experience this state more often in order to practice it with ease. All around us in nature we observe flowers, plants, trees, and animals quietly existing without much sound at all. Can we imitate them in creating spaces of silence?

Prior to the first papal encyclical on the environment, many other church documents called us to respond to the cry of Earth. Previous popes also wrote about the climate crisis. This is not something new in

Catholic Church teachings. This "new way of being" for Catholics is in harmony with many years of teaching. Let us imagine what this new way of being looks like in reality.

- What would it look like for us to spend more time with nature? By taking more walks through the woods, along the ocean, near a lake, along a river, we may slow ourselves down to listen more deeply.

- "Being" is something we have forgotten to practice. By just calming down while listening to soft music we are attending to our inner spirit. Take time for yourself as the catechist to quietly ponder nature prior to your class.

- In your car, you may want to listen to instrumental music that soothes your spirit while in traffic.

SUGGESTIONS FOR FAITH FORMATION

- Invite the children to create a special prayer space for themselves. Offer ideas for what that might include, such as favorite images of God, a flower, or a candle. They can write or draw a description of this and then take it home to share with their families.

- Invite the children to listen to instrumental music while they draw a picture of Jesus as they imagine him with them at this moment. Where are they sitting? What are they thinking? How does Jesus speak to them?

- Suggest that the children use their prayer space each night before they go to bed to kneel down to say their night prayers.

SUGGESTIONS FOR FAMILIES

- Create a family space for sitting in silence in your home. Add religious symbols, candle, colorful cloth, quiet instrumental music, and a comfortable chair. Encourage family members to take time to visit this space and to respect the space when others occupy it.

- Use this space for quiet prayer and meditation for family prayers. Pope Francis suggests that we pray the Rosary for care for creation.

- Make a prayer bowl or box that can be used to hold the pieces of paper that have your prayer petitions written on them. When you go to pray in quiet, read one or two of the prayer petitions and pray for it.

PRAYER

Beloved One, you are my hope in times of distress. I come to you to ask your help. Please speak to me now. Amen.

twenty-two

Ways to celebrate the joy and peace of our common home

Christian spirituality proposes a growth marked by moderation and the capacity to be happy with little. **LS, 222**

REFLECTION FOR CATECHISTS

Pope Francis says, "A constant flood of new consumer goods can baffle the heart and prevent us from cherishing each thing and each moment." The pope is reminding us to live more simply. Jesus has told us only one thing is necessary: to love. How do you try to live more simply?

When have you experienced joy in nature? Perhaps you could take a walk in the woods or by a lake, river, or ocean, or a public park. Reflect on how the trees, water, or plants help you to be quiet and calm. This feeling of calm and harmony is often missing in our lives. We need times of serenity to hear God's whisper in our hearts. The virtue of temperance helps us to refrain from surrounding ourselves with too much of anything. For example, too much food makes us ill. When we have "just enough" we feel content. Contentment helps us to be happy.

SUGGESTIONS FOR FAITH FORMATION

- Earth Day (April 22) is a special day to remind us about how special our common home is for all living beings on this planet. Download materials about Earth Day to share with your class and to inspire a class project around caring for our common home.

- Research how Earth Day came to be. How is it celebrated around the world?

- Talk to students about moderation and its relationship to living simply. For example, when eating we take "just enough" to satisfy our hunger. We stop and ask ourselves, "Am I hungry?" or "Am I eating just because the food is there?" Invite the children to name other instances where they can practice moderation.

SUGGESTIONS FOR FAMILIES

- Create a banner for Sunday. Make it a reminder for this day to be a day of joy and peace. See how you can safeguard time on Sunday to do things as a family (i.e., go for a nature walk together, go for ice cream together, take a ride, etc.).

- Living simply in our families can mean we look for ways to enjoy each other without needing to spend money. For example, we go for a picnic outdoors or pack a lunch and sit by a river or in a park rather than go to a restaurant. Living simply as a family can mean we show our appreciation for the one who cooks our meals by volunteering to wash the dishes and clean up after the meal.

PRAYER

God of peace and joy, help us to become more like you in our everyday life. Help us to see the joy in each other and the little things we do together. Amen.

twenty-three

How does the mystery of the Holy Trinity help us to care for our common home?

Everything is interconnected, and this invites us to develop a spirituality of that global solidarity which flows from the mystery of the Trinity. **LS, 240**

REFLECTION FOR CATECHISTS

In ***Laudato Si'***, Pope Francis says, "The Father is the ultimate source of everything...The Son, his reflection, through whom all things were created, united himself to this earth when he was formed in the womb of Mary. The Spirit, infinite bond of love, is intimately present at the very heart of the universe, inspiring and bringing new pathways" (238). In other words, although our God is One, there are three Persons in the one God. Each of these persons is a unique expression of the one Divinity, and they are all divine. As reflections of God, we, too, have unique expressions of God by how we live the love of God within us. In nature we see reflected God's beauty, enormous endurance, capacity for unconditional love, and suffering for our sake.

Remember, this is a mystery of our faith and cannot be fully understood. What can be understood is that the nature of God is a community of three Divine Persons, and we can imitate the communal nature of God in our ways of being in our families, parish, and world.

In other words, we are all one family of God! We need to live as one family in loving care for every member.

SUGGESTIONS FOR FAITH FORMATION

- The doctrine of the Holy Trinity is a mystery of our Catholic faith. A lesson we can live from this doctrine is community. The three Persons in one God live in perfect harmony. This is a model for our living community in harmony. To do this, we need to practice our communication skills.

- Practice communications skills, such as active listening, by dividing into groups of twos. One person in the group tells a story about something that happened to him or her. The other person listens. Then, they switch. When both have had a turn, each person repeats the story back to the other person to see if they got it right. If they did they were truly listening.

- One way to help active listening is to repeat back to the person who is speaking what you hear them saying. For instance, "I heard you say _____. Is that correct?" If you got it right the person will say "Yes." If you didn't, they can correct your understanding. Take turns explaining to one another how your day has gone so far.

- The Trinity gives us a model for community in families. Every family needs to learn how to live in harmony. Learning good communication skills helps every family become more loving as a whole. No matter how hard it might be to understand those who may have different opinions, it is always important to respect and to love the person. Imagine how God loves each person.

- For example, when we speak as a group we can remember that speaking about an idea is not the same as speaking about the person who has the idea. The idea is not the person. The idea is out on the table by itself apart from the person. You can illustrate this concept by using a brightly colored cloth as the idea. One person begins by holding the cloth as they speak. When they complete their thought about the topic, they place the cloth in the middle of the circle. Another person in the group who wants to respond picks up the cloth and speaks. This goes on until the end of the discussion.

- Ideas, opinions, and expressions may differ, but loving and reverencing each other is the foundation for family love.

- Practice the art of keeping silent when the other person is speaking. It helps to make eye contact. Look at the other person's eyes once in a while. Reflect back to them what you heard and be sure they agree it is what they meant to say. Sometimes our understanding turns out to differ from what the other meant when they spoke.

PRAYER

Holy Trinity of God, give us the graces we need to live in love as a family. We thank you for giving us the example of your loving community. Help us to imitate your loving unity. Amen.

twenty-four

How do I celebrate the Sabbath?

Since on the seventh day God was finished with the work he had been doing, he rested on the seventh day from all the work he had undertaken. So God blessed the seventh day and made it holy. GENESIS 2:2-3

REFLECTION FOR CATECHISTS

The Sabbath is a sign of the rest that God took after having created all that is. We give glory to God by giving rest to our body, mind, and spirit so that we can continue to learn and be our best selves for each other and for all that God desires of us. Rest comes in many forms. Restoration of body, mind, and spirit can happen every day, but Sunday is a good day to focus on this restoration. For example, you may want to schedule food shopping for Saturday or another day so that you do not need to do it on Sunday.

SUGGESTIONS FOR FAITH FORMATION

- Explain that, in the Catholic tradition, Sunday is the Sabbath day. In some countries, the family spends Sunday together. Our

Catholic tradition includes participation in the eucharistic liturgy as the best way to celebrate the Sabbath. As a church, we believe we are the body of Christ. We commemorate the dying and rising of Jesus Christ, the head of the body, through the eucharistic liturgy. This is what we call Mass.

- Invite the students to share what they do as a family on Sundays. If they have not done anything special in the past, what would be a good idea to suggest to their family now?

SUGGESTIONS FOR FAMILIES

- Plan a family outing for Sundays so you can better enjoy each other as a family.

- Create a special meal for Sunday to celebrate the Sabbath.

- Dress up in special clothes to celebrate the Sabbath.

- As a family, visit a homebound person in your parish on Sunday. Take a parish bulletin to them.

- Write cards that say "Thinking of you" to parishioners who are on the sick and homebound list in your parish bulletin.

- As a family, make it your intention to break the habit of using cell phones so much, and decide that you want to be in touch in a more personal way. Try to turn off your electronic devices for at least a few hours each Sunday.

PRAYER

Loving Maker of all that is, we praise and thank you this day for the beauty of nature. We ask you to help us to relax, to rest our minds and nurture our spirits so that we can become our best selves and love each other more deeply. Amen.

twenty-five

What sacramental signs help us to remember to care for our common home?

"This is the sign that I am giving for all ages to come of the covenant between me and the earth. When I bring clouds over the earth, and the bow appears in the clouds..." **GENESIS 9:12-14**

REFLECTION FOR CATECHISTS

Sacramentals are symbols or signs that remind us of our faith in God and help us feel close to God. For example, the rosary or a medal of a saint are sacramentals, the Sign of the Cross and holy water are sacramentals. Our "common home," Earth, also reflects God. We lose part of the reflection of God when Earth is damaged or destroyed. So, when we see trash polluting a river or the beauty of nature in a park, we can be reminded to restore the beauty by picking up the trash and putting it where it belongs. We do not think of this as something "set apart" for the honor of God but because nature is a reflection of God. Seeing nature abused or blemished reminds us to do our part in restoring the beauty God had in mind when creating it.

- Explain how the rainbow is God's sign of the covenant of love between God and Noah. What else can a rainbow remind us of? For example, a rainbow reminds us of the many different colors there are in nature, in humans, in all life. It is a sign of diversity. Guide the class in creating a mural of a rainbow to show the beauty of differences in creation. Cut out photos of nature from magazines. Arrange them in a collage to hang as a reminder of the beauty of nature.

- Assist the students in praying the Rosary using the Mysteries of Creation. These are listed on the website *thecatholicspirit.com*. Write the names of the mysteries on a whiteboard or flip chart and invite the children to create prayer stations for each one. Suggest that children make up their own mysteries of the Rosary for care for creation. Invite them to draw a symbol for each mystery. For example, the mysteries could be

  1. The stars are created;
  2. All the galaxies are created;
  3. Our solar system is created;
  4. Water fills the seas;
  5. Land appears on our common home.

SUGGESTIONS FOR FAMILIES

- Name some sacramentals that you have in your home to remind you of God, the Blessed Mother, and the saints. For example: a crucifix, statues, rosary, blessed palm, holy water, or pictures of saints.

- What do you have that reminds you of creation and caring for our common home? For example, if possible, make a terrarium as a family. A terrarium is an enclosed garden that needs very little attention to keep it going. Invite a family member to research what you need to make a terrarium for the family.

- What other species besides human do you have in your home? How do you show your care for them? For example, do you have a pet? What is it that you do to care for your pet?

- As a family, create a collage of your favorite photos of nature and the beauty of creation. Frame your collage for all to appreciate.

- If you have traveled to a beautiful place on vacation, frame a picture that reminds you of the trip and how you want to be sure it remains beautiful for those who come after you.

PRACTICE

PRAYER

Creator of all things, we desire to be good caregivers of this one Earth, our home. Help us to see you in all that lives. Amen.

twenty-six

What can we do during Advent to care for our common home?

Living our vocation to be protectors of God's handiwork is essential to a life of virtue; it is not an optional or a secondary aspect of our Christian experience. **LS, 217**

REFLECTION FOR CATECHISTS

Advent is a perfect time for Catholics to live "our vocation to be protectors of God's handiwork." Advent gives us the opportunity to create a calendar of simplicity. How will we create a celebration of Christmas that is a witness to our faith and values? We pray to be less materialistic and simpler in our gift-giving, decorating, and feasting. Prayer becomes easier when we are not distracted by too much "stuff."

SUGGESTIONS FOR FAITH FORMATION

- Engage the children in making a Christmas crèche from a cardboard cereal box and clothespins or corks for the people. Paint the figures and stable. Draw in straw, window, cow, etc. Place an angel on top.

- Pope Francis mentions how important it is to reduce our consumerism and materialism. Discuss ways to make gifts to give to loved ones instead of purchasing so much. For example, is it possible to use recycled materials to create bookmarks, eyeglass holders, cell phone holders, candy boxes, etc.?

- Use recycled materials to create greeting cards to deliver to people who are in nursing homes. Check with the parish staff about ways to deliver the cards through home visitors or extraordinary ministers of Holy Communion.

SUGGESTIONS FOR FAMILIES

- Hang an Advent calendar on the refrigerator and check off what you do as a family to prepare for Christmas by also caring for God's creation.

- How can you increase the amount of biodegradable materials you use to wrap presents? For example, you can use cloth material or comics from the newspaper to wrap gifts. Try to give gifts that are consumable so as to keep from adding to the landfill.

- Think of giving plants as gifts. For example, you can give bulbs and a bowl of stones. Add a small amount of water to the stones. Place the bulbs on the stones. Watch them grow during the dark month of January.

- If you use candles, use soy based ones to minimize the amount of carbon you're putting in the atmosphere.

PRAYER

Loving One who came to Earth to be one of us and one with us, we pray that we may imitate your simplicity and spirit of poverty. We are important in your eyes just because we are! We thank you for your great love. Amen.

twenty-seven

What can we do during Lent to care for our common home?

Remember that you are dust and to dust you shall return.

ASH WEDNESDAY PRAYER FOR PLACING ASHES ON THE FOREHEAD

REFLECTION FOR CATECHISTS

The words we hear when we receive ashes on Ash Wednesday help us to remember that we are so much a part of Earth that, like ashes, we are made of the soil and will return to soil when we die. Death is a mystery. We do not know all there is to know about what happens after we die. What we do know and believe by faith is that we will, like Jesus, rise again in the resurrection of the body. That is why we, as Catholics, take such care of the body in life and also in death.

Jesus gave us an example of love without measure. He chose to die rather than to cause any harm. The crucifix is a symbol of his unconditional love for us.

- Invite the children to compose a prayer to God for our Earth. For example, "Dear God, thank you for the beauty of our Earth. Help us to live in such a way as to add to that beauty and not take away from it with pollution."

- Help the children make crosses out of sticks found in a nature walk. Wrap them together with purple yarn. Use this cross as a reminder of Lent. Encourage them to say their prayer with this cross each night before they get into bed. For example, they might say a prayer like this: "Dear God, thank you for this day. Bless (*name each person in your family*) this night and keep them safe from harm. Amen."

- Lent is a time for prayer, fasting, and almsgiving. Ask them for some ways they can make the connection between caring for creation and these three lenten activities. For example, invite the children to make up a prayer for protection of creation with a lenten theme; or suggest that the children think of something to give up that would have a positive effect on our Earth, for example, to use less paper or water, or to eat less meat. Invite the class to donate whatever they can to a local food pantry or soup kitchen. This could be either nonperishable foods or money donations.

- The church requires us to go without meat on the Fridays of Lent. Donate the money you save by doing this to the National Rice Bowl collection in church. (Catholic Relief Services offers the Rice Bowl as a program in parishes. See their website: *www.CRS.org*.)

- Go to the website of Catholic Relief Services for ideas to pray, fast, and give alms during Lent.

- Decide as a family how you want to practice something special for Lent.

- Create a lenten corner for the family. Place in it a prayer box that contains slips of paper describing the acts of kindness you want to practice during Lent. Every day, pick one that gives you an idea of how to practice loving kindness for that day.

- As a family, pray the Rosary together after supper for all those who have no food, shelter, or clothing.

- As a family, plant a bush or a tree that reminds you of the beauty of creation.

- Fast from using fossil fuels for part of Lent. For example, walk instead of driving a car once a week.

PRAYER

Loving God, thank you for the example of your Son, Jesus. He died on the cross rather than act in an unloving way. Help us to look at you and to practice loving kindness every day. Amen.

twenty-eight

Mary, our Blessed Mother, Queen of Creation, is a model for us to care for our common home

She is the Woman, "clothed in the sun, with the moon under her feet, and on her head a crown of twelve stars." **LS, 241**

REFLECTION FOR CATECHISTS

At the conclusion of *Laudato Si'*, Pope Francis reminds us that Mary is now transfigured and lives with Jesus. She is "carried up to heaven" and is "Mother and Queen of all creation." We pray to Mary to intercede for us with her Son, Jesus, in helping us to keep our Earth beautiful. Pope Francis says we can ask Mary to help us to look at our world with eyes of wisdom so that we can understand how to care for God's creation. Mary is seen as glorious and set apart because she was to become the Mother of God. However, her life was not extraordinary in her everyday tasks. She did what any other woman of Nazareth did to keep a home for their family. We know her life was simple and that she knew the Scriptures. Other than that we know very little. It is easy to imagine Mary lovingly tending the home in ways that made it comfortable for Jesus and Joseph.

Since she cared for the body of Christ when he was on this earth, she now cares for the body of Christ in our world, the church suffering in its members all over the world. Like Mary, we need to care for those affected most by severe climate changes. Everything and everyone is connected. Mary is a model of compassionate love. She is our model for loving kindness.

SUGGESTIONS FOR FAITH FORMATION

- Provide a place in your teaching space for a statue of Mary.

- Explain that, like Mary, Catholics care for each other by sharing what we have. For example, we might donate gently used clothes, toys, and other items to organizations that help those in need. We might also decide not to purchase so many new items. This reduces the spirit of consumerism so prevalent in our society today.

- Like Mary, may we act with love and gentleness when we speak with others. Kindness reflects Mary's manner of being. As Catholics, we have a special devotion to Mary, the Mother of God, queen of all creation. We use only words of loving kindness and never hurtful words. Give examples of how this looks in your classroom. For example, use the words "please," "thank you," "I am sorry," and "please excuse me."

SUGGESTIONS FOR FAMILIES

- Declutter your clothes closets and, like Mary, be simple in your manner of dress.

- Declutter your closets and give what you do not really need to a local thrift shop.

- How are you able to imitate Mary in her compassion for those who are suffering, like her Son, today? Be a listening ear for someone who is suffering within your family.

- Earth is suffering today. How can you, like Mary, be one who hears the cry of our suffering Earth? We have learned that people who are materially poor are the ones who will suffer the most from severe climate changes. This is due to a lack of resources for survival and access to transportation to move from the affected locations. We can become more sensitive to the effects of severe weather patterns by reducing the amount of carbon dioxide we put into the atmosphere. This is called our "carbon footprint." The Catholic Climate Covenant (*www.catholicclimatecovenant.org*) asks us, "Who is under your carbon footprint?"

PRAYER

Mary, Queen of all Creation, we honor you as we pray for deeper compassion for our suffering Earth. Help us to be more active as caregivers for her and for those who are poor and suffering from severe weather. Amen.

twenty-nine

What saints are good examples of caring for our common home?

Start by doing what's necessary; then do what's possible; and suddenly you are doing the impossible.

ATTRIBUTED TO ST. FRANCIS OF ASSISI

REFLECTION FOR CATECHISTS

A "saint" is a holy person, someone declared by the Catholic Church to be in heaven. In addition to this, we know there are people whom we have known who have lived or are living holy lives. These are people who look for ways to live good, simple lives in a humble, patient, and charitable manner. They are persistent in doing good without reward. For example, the mother of six children who teaches her children how to pray, how to recycle, how to conserve water, is saintly. Living an environmentally sustainable life is not easy. If we do it united to the God of creation and with a patient heart, we too can be called saints.

In order to become "holy," we need to practice inconvenience in our society, which holds convenience in such high regard. Sometimes the convenient way hurts our common home, Earth. By going the "extra mile" as Jesus suggested, we are becoming saints today!

SUGGESTIONS FOR FAITH FORMATION

- St. Francis of Assisi is the patron saint of ecology. Read a story of his life to understand why he is called this. Show a brief DVD of his life in class.

- In the life of St. Martin de Porres we learn how kind he was to all of God's creatures. Tell his story to the children and invite them to write about ways to show concern for all of God's creatures.

- St. Kateri Tekawitha is a Native American saint. What other stories of Native Americans give us good examples of how to care for Earth?

- Create a skit about the lives or life of one or more saints to perform for the group.

- Create a song about one of the saints.

SUGGESTIONS FOR FAMILIES

- All Saints Day Eve is called Halloween. It is a day to honor the saints. Look into dressing your child as one of the saints that cared for God's creation.

- Make a costume from recycled materials for Halloween.

- Create a book with illustrations of these saints that shows care for our common home.

- Read bedtime stories about the saints to your family.

PRAYER

Loving God, with all the saints we praise and thank you for the many varied ways you give us examples of how to care for our common home. Give us the courage and grace to do so each day. Amen.

thirty

Canticle of the Sun: Ways to celebrate Earth every day

Let us sing as we go. May our struggles and our concern for this planet never take away the joy of our hope. **LS, 244**

REFLECTION FOR CATECHISTS

St. Francis of Assisi praised God, our Creator, with his Canticle of the Sun, a prayer that has been put to song. As Pope Francis says in his encyclical, we should join together to sing our praises to God for the gifts of creation as well as to commit ourselves to care for the Earth, our common home.

Joy in hope is the message we must keep in our hearts. Others will appreciate the effects of such a joy from us. Our actions done in joy are a witness of our Catholic faith. Pope Francis speaks of the "joy of the gospel" in his writings. We, like him, must live the gospel in a spirit of joy and compassion. Everyone will see the fruits of joy in the actions we take to care for our common home together.

SUGGESTIONS FOR FAITH FORMATION

- Find music for the Canticle of the Sun in parish songbooks or on a CD and teach it to the children. Sing or say the words to the canticle as you form a class procession to walk around the outside of the church.

- Use the words of Canticle to the Sun for an art project. Distribute paper and markers and invite children to illustrate one of their favorite lines from the canticle. Post the pictures in the parish hall.

- Invite the children to join together in making up gestures for the Canticle of the Sun. Then read it while the children act out the gestures.

SUGGESTIONS FOR FAMILIES

- Shorten the original version of the Canticle to use as a night prayer before going to bed.

- Create a sun catcher that illustrates the Canticle of the Sun. Hang it in a window as a reminder to praise God for creation and to care for it.

- Pope Francis calls us to remember to pray before and after meals. Use the Canticle of the Sun to do this.

PRAYER

O Loving Creator God, we thank you for the beauty of creation. We know how precious it is in your sight. Help us by your grace to become more deeply in love with all of creation. Amen.

Family Resources Center
415 NE Monroe
Peoria, IL 61603 (309) 839-2287